# BEN'S DREAM

## STORY AND PICTURES BY CHRIS VAN ALLSBURG

HOUGHTON MIFFLIN COMPANY    BOSTON

# To Valerie

Walter Lorraine *wλ* Books

For information about this and other Houghton Mifflin trade
and reference books and multimedia products, visit the Bookstore
at Houghton Mifflin on the World Wide Web at
http://www.hmco.com/trade/.

*Library of Congress Cataloging in Publication Data*
Van Allsburg, Chris.
Ben's dream.

Summary: On a terrifically rainy day, Ben has a dream
in which he and his house float by the monuments of the
world, half submerged in flood water.
RNF  ISBN  0-395-32084-4      PAP   ISBN   0-395-87470-X
[1.  Dreams–Fiction.     2.  Floods–Fiction]     1.  Title.
PZ7.V266Be     [Fic]      81-20029
AACR2

Printed in the United States of America
WOZ  20

# BEN'S DREAM

Ben and Margaret pedaled faster when they saw the black rain clouds rolling in. They had hoped to play baseball with some friends that afternoon.

"I guess," said Margaret, "I'll go home and study for that geography test tomorrow."

"Me too," answered Ben, as he turned his bike down the road that led to his house. "See you later."

Ben's mother was not home. He went into the living room and sat in his father's easy chair, opening his school book to study for the geography test on great landmarks of the world.

As Ben read, rain began to fall against the window—lightly at first, then a steady downpour heavier than Ben had ever seen. The rhythmic sound of the rain drumming on the window made him a little sleepy. In fact, very sleepy.

But then . . .

Ben opened his eyes. The room was full of sunshine. The storm had passed. Margaret was at the window.

"Hey, Ben, wake up," she yelled again.

Ben opened the window.

"Come on, sleepyhead, we're going to play baseball."

Ben grabbed his mitt and ran outside. He and Margaret walked their bikes down Ben's rough gravel driveway.

"You know," Margaret said, "that geography book put me to sleep too. And I had the funniest dream. I floated around the world past all those landmarks. They were half under water. You'll never guess who I saw when I floated past the Sphinx."

Ben smiled. "Me," he said, "standing on my front porch, waving."

Margaret's jaw dropped in amazement. "Gosh, how did you know?"

Ben got on his bike and pedaled ahead. "Because I saw you there!" he called out, and rolled down the hill.

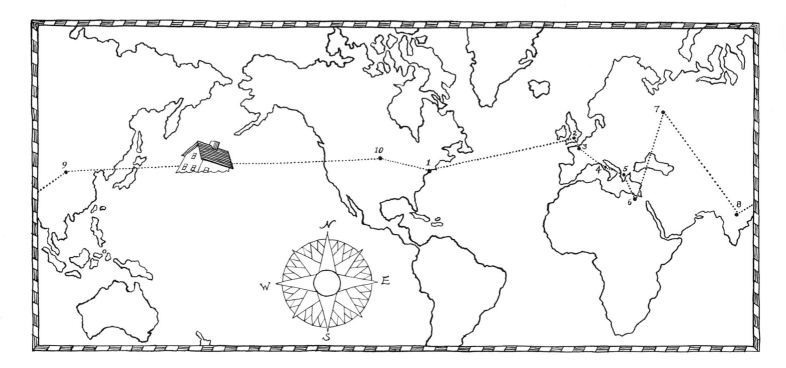

Here are the monuments from Ben's dream.

1. Pages 10–11. The Statue of Liberty (New York). Built in 1886 by the French architect Bartholdi. 151 feet tall.

2. Pages 12–13. Big Ben (London). This tower, built in 1860, was named for the bell that it houses.

3. Pages 14–15. The Eiffel Tower (Paris). Designed by Gustave Eiffel for the 1889 World's Fair. 1,056 feet tall.

4. Pages 16–17. The Tower of Pisa (Italy). Built in the twelfth through fourteenth centuries, today it leans 7.5 feet.

5. Pages 18–19. The Parthenon (Athens). Marble temple erected for the goddess Athena on the Acropolis in the fifth century B.C.

6. Pages 20–21. The Sphinx (Egypt). Fabled creature with the body of a lion and head of a pharaoh, carved from a block of limestone 70 feet high. It stands guard in front of the pyramids.

7. Pages 22–23. Basilica of St. Basil the Blessed (Moscow). Built by Ivan the Terrible in the sixteenth century near the Kremlin to celebrate his victory over the Tartars.

8. Pages 24–25. The Taj Mahal (India). Marble palace built in Agra between 1632 and 1654 by the emperor Châh Jahan for his wife. Today it is still one of the most beautiful buildings in India.

9. Pages 26–27. The Great Wall of China. A wall more than 3,600 miles long built in the third century B.C. to protect the Chinese from barbarian invasions.

10. Pages 28–29. Mount Rushmore (United States). The gigantic faces of four American presidents are carved in this mountain: Washington, Jefferson, Roosevelt, and Lincoln.